Instagram For Business

Unleash The Power Of Instagram With A Step-by-Step Guide For Your First 10,000 Followers And Learn The Ways To Monetize Them!

© Copyright 2018

All rights reserved.

The content contained within this book may not be reproduced, duplicated or transmitted without direct written permission from the author or the publisher.

Under no circumstances will any blame or legal responsibility be held against the publisher, or author, for any damages, reparation, or monetary loss due to the information contained within this book. Either directly or indirectly.

Legal Notice:

This book is copyright protected. This book is only for personal use. You cannot amend, distribute, sell, use, quote or paraphrase any part, or the content within this book, without the consent of the author or publisher.

Disclaimer Notice:

Please note the information contained within this document is for educational and entertainment purposes only. All effort has been executed to present accurate, up to date, and reliable, complete information. No warranties of any kind are declared or implied. Readers acknowledge that the author is not engaging in the rendering of legal, financial, medical or professional advice. The content within this book has been derived from various sources. Please consult a licensed professional before attempting any techniques outlined in this book.

By reading this document, the reader agrees that under no circumstances are is the author responsible for any losses, direct or indirect, which are incurred as a result of the use of information contained within this document, including, but not limited to, —errors, omissions, or inaccuracies.

Table of Contents

Preference *6*
   Who can Use this Book? *7*
Chapter One: Introduction *8*
   Instagram Features and Tools. *9*
   Instagram App Layout *12*
   Bottom Buttons, from Left to Right *13*
   Why Instagram for your Business? *14*
   Instagram Monetization *16*
   Instagram for Business Tools *17*
Chapter Two: Building Value and Setting Up Your Account for Success *20*
   Steps in Setting Up Instagram for Business *21*
   Importance of an Instagram Business Account *28*
   Building Value for your Instagram Business Account ... *31*
   Attract your Competitors' followers to your Account ... *34*
   Ways to Monetize Your Instagram Following *40*
Chapter 3: Going Viral *45*
   How do you go viral? *45*
Chapter 4: Instagram DM Groups *50*
   How do Instagram DM Groups work? *51*
   Joining Instagram DM Groups *51*
   DM Groups on Instagram *52*
   Instagram Groups on Telegram *53*
Chapter Five: Branding, Selling & Buying Accounts ... *55*
   Branding Instagram Accounts *55*
   Buying and Selling Instagram Accounts *58*

Chapter Six: Instagram Stories, IG Live, and Call to Action *63*
   Instagram Stories *63*
   IG Live *67*
   Call to Action on Instagram *70*
Chapter Seven: Affiliate Marketing through Instagram *74*
   Affiliate Marketing on Instagram *75*
Chapter Eight: How to Make Money with Shoutouts ... *78*
   How Much Money can you Generate per Shoutout? *80*
   How Effective are Instagram Shoutouts? *80*
Chapter Nine: Best Apps to Use to Market your Brand on Instagram *81*
   Best Photo Editing Apps *81*
   Best Graphic Design Apps *83*
   Best Instagram Account Management App *84*
   Best Video Recording App *85*
Conclusion *87*
Thank you for Buying this Book. *89*

Preference

Launched in October 2010 on iOS platforms and April 2012 for Android devices, Instagram has drastically evolved from an app for just sharing selfies and photos to a social media marketing tool essential for any business with an ambition. With over 400 million users, with more than 80 million posts daily coupled with over 94% monthly, the power of Instagram in marketing a business cannot be overlooked and must be embraced by any business looking to expand its market globally.

Additionally, Instagram has released more enhanced futures enabling business enterprises not only focused on brand awareness through advertisements but also influential marketing, product promotion, and other features. I, therefore, came up with this book to enable business enterprises to learn and embrace Instagram for marketing as it is essential for a business to build a presence on Instagram. In the book, we deeply analyze

Instagram for business, highlighting the ways of setting up an account, gaining and monetizing the first 10,000 followers. We will also discuss the latest Instagram features for business, including Instagram stories and hashtags and how a business can utilize these features to market their products.

Who can Use this Book?

This book can be used by business enterprises who wish to learn about the power of Instagram in marketing their business. The book features a step-by-step guide to setting up an Instagram account and gaining enough followers who can be monetized. Additionally, the latest Instagram features tailored specifically for marketing a business are also discussed in the book. It is therefore expected that after going through the book, one can implement what they have learned from the book in their businesses enterprises to realize increased profit margins due to an enlarged market credit because of an active Instagram presence.

Chapter One: Introduction

Instagram was developed by Mike Krieger and Kevin Systrom in San Francisco while they were focusing on their HTML5 multi-featured project. After years of development, Kevin Systrom was the first person to post pictures on Instagram on July 16, 2010, but it wasn't until October 6, 2010 that Instagram was officially released on iOS devices through the App Store. Instagram was released for Android platforms on April 3, 2012 with more than a million downloads on the first day of release and on Windows platforms on November 21, 2013, through a beta version of the app, though the app could not record or upload a video due to incomplete development. Instagram was upgraded to support video and direct messaging on Windows 10 Mobile in April 2016 and Window 10 tablets and personal computers in October 2016. To date, Instagram has been purchased by Facebook and has undergone two major updates and a facelift on its design featuring a modern colorful icon with a black-and-white theme in the app display on May 11, 2016.

Instagram Features and Tools.

Instagram has several features designed to enhance the sharing of videos and images over the platform. Users can upload videos and images with an option to indicate the location of the image posted through a geotag. Privacy is also enhanced through a "privacy" option which limits only a user's followers to view their images. Integration with other social media, platforms including Facebook, Twitter, Tumbril and Flickr, allows users to share their images or videos through a single post on Instagram eliminating the need of double posting. The hashtag feature enables accumulation specific images or videos to make images easily locatable or stand out attracting concurring Instagram users. Users can upload full-size or portrait photos and videos with an option to enhance them through an inbuilt photo editing app, which improves photos through new and live filters, instant tilt-shift, high-resolution photographs, one-click rotation, optional borders and an updated icon. The zoom feature allows users to zoom in on photos and videos. Users can save photos and videos in an organized collection like a photo album for later viewing through the bookmark feature.

Users can upload up to ten images or videos which can easily be accessed by other users by swiping left or right through a swipeable carousel. The archive features enable users to hide posts out of the visibility of the public or other users in a private storage area. Users can comment on the posts of other users with the comments organized in a thread, enabling users to interact more easily through replies conveyed in real-time.

The explore tab feature allows users to discover photos taken at a nearby location or based on liked photos by a user or recent searches. The explore tab also features trending tags and places, curated content, and the ability to search for post location. Instagram added additional features to the Explore Tab including a "Videos You Might Like" and "Events" channel, allowing users to view videos from latest sports games, concerts and other live events happening around the world. The Instagram Live tab allows users to access an algorithmically-curated page of the best Instagram Live videos currently on air. The Explore tab promotes public Stories content from nearby places.

Instagram Direct allows users to interact with each other through private messaging. Users who follow each other can send private messages with videos and photos to a maximum of fifteen users. The feature was also enhanced with additional conversation threads, making it possible for users to share locations, hashtag pages, and profiles through private messages directly from the news feed. Users are also able to reply to private messages through texts, emojis or by clicking a heart emoji. Additionally, website links can be sent in messages with the addition of sending photos in their original portrait or landscape orientation without cropping.

The Instagram stories feature, launched in August 2016, allows users to upload photos which can be enhanced through effects and layers on their story timelines. The images or videos uploaded to the storyline timeline automatically expire after 24 hours. Users can also add their live broadcasts to their storyline timelines with an option to respond to stories by sending messages, photos and videos complete with Instagram effects such as filters, stickers, and hashtags.

Instagram App Layout

After opening the app, the home screen is first displayed with the following buttons

Top Buttons

***Camera Button(camera)*-** The button is directly linked to your device camera and by touching it, you start sharing photos and videos either from the photo gallery or take a quick snap or record a video and upload it in real time.

Direct messages (paper airplane)- This tab notifies the user of a private message. A user can also send a private message to other users by clicking on this tab.

Bottom Buttons, from Left to Right

Home Button (House)- By clicking on this button, users can view the latest videos and photos posted by other users from accounts they follow.

Search Button (Magnifying glass)- The search button basically allows users to explore top accounts, people, places, hashtags, videos or other content or account suggested to them based on their recently liked content or followed accounts.

Camera (Square with plus sign)- Users can upload to their accounts and share photos and videos by tapping on this button.

Notifications(heart)- This tab updates users of recent activities in their accounts including recent likes and comments on your posts or even activities for people they follow.

Profile (circular photo)- This tab contains all a user's posts, including the profile photo with the profile information. Also, users get access to the setting menu where they can change the privacy setting of their account, change the profile picture with the profile information or other settings tailored to meet their account needs.

Why Instagram for your Business?

As stated in the previous subtopic, Instagram is a social media platform designed to share photos and videos developed in 2010. Instagram has undergone immense growth since its inception with over 800 million active users currently, 200 million more than Twitter and other social media platforms. Additionally, a study established that one out of four American adults is actually active on Instagram, therefore its effectiveness as a marketing tool cannot be ignored.

With a growing number of users, Instagram offers exceptional features absent on other social media platforms such as Twitter and Facebook. Users can easily navigate through posted videos and photos without missing any content posted by a business. Additionally, business accounts can post more than ten pictures or videos of their products in a simple and visually stunning way to draw users who can swipe left or right as the content appears in a swipeable carousel. And as an additional feature, the app is impeccably incorporated with other social media platforms including Facebook, Twitter, Tumbril and Flickr to seamlessly share content to users on these other social media platforms without having to post more than twice. To further understand the impact of Instagram on a business, let's discuss Instagram monetization products.

Instagram Monetization

Instagram announced that it would increase its monetization efforts by integrating video and image ads in between a user's posted photos in the news feed in October 2013. The ads would feature a text "Sponsored" at the top right of the image under the news feed but only a limited number of brands were allowed to advertise at that particular stage exclusively in America. By September 2014, Instagram had rolled out image advertisements in Australia, Canada, and the United Kingdom

Instagram further improved its monetization policies by allowing advertisers to purchase "carousel ads," in which brands can combine their websites to up to five images or videos posted in March 2016. New additional features to enhance business advertisements were launched in May 2016, which included newly improved business profiles, Insights analytics, and the option to convert posts into ads directly using Instagram. The Insight analytics panel allows users to view a business's top posts while a business can view their impressions, reach and engagement surrounding their post including user demographics. By March 2017, Instagram had over one million advertisers due to its universality and low cost of advertising, thereby making it a suitable social media platform to advertise a business's products or services.

Instagram for Business Tools

Instagram for business tools are designed to enable a business to efficiently use Instagram business accounts to market their brands. Although some tools are still under development, the tools work perfectly for Instagram business accounts that numerous companies are taking advantage of Instagram advertising to expand beyond their current markets and find new customers across the globe. Below are some of the tools used in Instagram business accounts.

1. Business profiles

This is a free feature in which accounts can recognize themselves as a business on Instagram. By using business profiles, businesses can upload information deemed appropriate for the convenience of customers such as location, phone number, website link as well as directions. Followers can then have an easy time while contacting the business through calling, texting, emailing or even visiting their webpage by just tapping on the contact button. Additionally, a business profile is necessary to unlock other business tools including insights and the ability to promote.

2. Insights

Insight is a business tool which enables businesses to access vital information, also referred to as metrics, about their accounts and followers i.e. demographics, geographical location, behavior, and which posts are suited to the followers more than others. There are two ways to view the metrics – on the overall account dashboard and on each post itself via impressions, reach and engagement. Impressions are how many times each post has been viewed by Instagram users. Reach refers to how many unique user accounts viewed a post while engagement refers to how many unique accounts liked or commentated on a post. With this information, a business can upload more relevant and timely content, which would go a long way toward opening the business's global market.

3. Promote

The promote tool enables a business to convert well-performing posts into adverts using the Instagram app, enabling it to connect with even more customers without incurring extra advertisement costs. How efficient is this? Based on the most liked or viewed post, you add a tab initiating followers or other users to act and buy or inquire about the brand. There is an option to select a target or allow Instagram to select the audience for the business based on analyzed statistics. The post will then be promoted as an advert for the period you select.

Chapter Two: Building Value and Setting Up Your Account for Success

To realize the full potential of Instagram for your business, the first step of course, is to set up a Business Instagram account, which is pretty different from the normal personalized accounts and offers additional features essential for your business marketing needs. With an increasing number of users daily, through your Instagram business accounts, you can share and attract millions of potential customers through graphically rich photos and videos portraying inspiring stories about your brand or business and why they should choose your business or brand over the rest in the global market.

Also, before setting up an Instagram account, it's important to have a strategy just like in your business plan. Ask yourself, what is the aim of setting up the Instagram business account? Possibly it could be to find new customers, expand the market for your products globally, promote a specific product to increase sales, share your company's culture that may be deemed satisfying to customers or even to discover and learn the latest trends in the industry that you can implement in your business. Whatever your aim, always have a clear strategy like a blueprint, as it will help you achieve your goal.

Steps in Setting Up Instagram for Business

Instagram works synonymously with Facebook, therefore you will need to have a business Facebook page setup before opening an Instagram business account and linking it to your Facebook page. Having a LinkedIn or Twitter account will be advantageous for your business as it will enable you to reach out to other prospective customers who may not be using Instagram or following your business account on Instagram

1. Download the Instagram app

Instagram is quite different from other social media platforms such as Facebook and Twitter since posting videos and photos can only be done through the Instagram app. Therefore, you will need to download from the in-app purchases section in the Play Store for Android devices and App Store for iOS devices. The file size is about 2.0 MB and you should not worry about the space on your device.

2. Using an Email Address to Create your Account

You should have an email address for your business prior to opening an Instagram account for your business. It is advisable to create an account based on the profile on your Facebook page or other social media account including Twitter and LinkedIn, as it will go a long way in ensuring prospective customers identify your business easily on all these social media platforms. Also, using a personal or work email address when setting up your business account will ensure that your contacts easily find you using the "Find Friends" tab feature.

3. Choose a Username

The next step will be to choose a username coupled with a password for security purpose. Always ensure that when choosing a username, it should be the company's name or a close variation. Also, if you are a real estate agent, salesperson, insurance agent or any agent, you should choose a username that closely ties with your personal name, location or business and differentiates your business account from your personal account. For instance, in the case of a real estate agent, Micheal Williams-NYC-realtor or Micheal Williams-LA-ins for the case of an insurance agent. Don't worry if you can't come up with a suitable name since Instagram can automatically generate a username based on the keyed profile name.

4. *Uploading a Profile Photo*

Your profile photo says a lot about your business or profession, therefore it is important to pick the right profile photo. The profile photo should be your business logo, or an easily recognizable sign associated with your brand. In the case of your business offering professional services, upload your professional headshot image donning professional attire, for example, a white coat in the case of medical professionals or a helmet and reflector jackets in the case of real estate agents or engineers.

To upload a profile photo, tap the "Add a photo" tab where you will be given several upload options including an option to upload a profile photo from Facebook or Twitter. You can upload your profile photo from other social media accounts if they are your business account. After uploading a profile photo, save your info by clicking "Done" located in the top right corner to eliminate the need for password inputs while logging in to your account and to accelerate future logins.

5. *Complete your Profile*

After uploading your profile photo, complete your profile by clicking on the "Edit Your Profile" button and filling the required fields, which are a name, username, website, bio, email, contact info and gender. The website field is significant for your business as it is the only section where your account visitors are automatically directed to your website after clicking on the URL. A URL posted in the comment section of a post is void and users may not be able to access your website through the URL posted.

The biofield is also limited to a few characters, therefore you must be brief in explaining the type of business, services or products offered, location, and why people should choose your brand over the rest.

6. *Switch to Instagram for Business.*

This is the most important step in setting up an Instagram business account as it distinguishes a personalized account from a business account and allows you to access Instagram for business tools, perfect for use by any business. In the "Edit Profile" page find and tap on the "Try Instagram Business Tools" button where you will automatically be directed settings in "Switch to business account tab." After clicking on the button, you will be required to upload information pertaining to your business including opening hours, phone number, and your business address. With an Instagram business account, you can access insights about your posts, stories, and even your account followers.

7. *Link your Business Instagram Account to your Business Facebook page.*

We already stated the need of having a Facebook business page to reach out to other prospective customers who may not be on Instagram. Instagram will automatically ask you to link your Facebook page to the created account. A Facebook business page is also important for you to use the Instagram for business tools.

8. Find Facebook friends & contacts.

After setting up an account and linking it to your business Facebook page, Instagram will automatically recommend people to follow based on your Facebook page followers or your contact information. You can skip this stage based on the strategy or idea of setting up an Instagram business page. For instance, maybe you would need a completely new market for your product or you do not prefer your contacts following your Instagram business page. In later topics, we are going to discuss building value for your business by gaining followers and monetizing them.

9. Start Posting

Start posting content deemed appropriate for your business field using relevant captions and hashtags.

Also, after posting, follow similar accounts who have tagged their contents using the same hashtag. Through hashtags, millions of photos are arranged in one virtual location like a database, thereby enabling users to easily locate accounts, thus your business account can easily be located by prospective customers, adding value to business marketing needs. Additionally, use popular hashtags such as #happy, #love, #tbt as they are used by millions of users thereby exposing your business for easy access by prospective customers. Use a specific hashtag, for instance, #realestate or #property if you are targeting a forte of customers.

Importance of an Instagram Business Account

- You can access real-time metrics on how your stories and promoted posts performed throughout the day, week or month

- With a business account, you can get insights into your followers and how they interact with your posts and stories
- You can add information relating to your company such as location, business hours and phone number, therefore it is convenient for your customers.
- With the swipe-up feature in the story timeline, you insert a link to redirect your followers to anywhere appropriate, be it your webpage or your YouTube channel, increasing your potential for sale conversion. This tool can be your oyster specifically if you have a business profile with over 10k followers.
- With an Instagram business account, you can legitimize your business creating an impression of legality in prospective customers. Highlighting your brand profile using an Instagram business account has turned out to be the ideal way of legitimizing your business, especially through the blue verification

checkmark. This, in turn, attracts numerous customers who would want to buy products or services from legitimate business as they are assured of the quality of the product or service being advertised.

- An Instagram business account enables you to utilize Instagram's native shopping function. This feature enables businesses with an Instagram business account to grow their brand by acquiring new customers who drive sales in very indirect ways. Most people on Instagram discover a product but may not purchase right there and then but would come back to purchase the product after maybe getting some cash. With this tool, users can obtain a lot more information relating to the product thereby assisting them in deciding to buy a product.

Building Value for your Instagram Business Account

The essence of creating an Instagram business account is to market your brand globally by uploading videos and photos of your brand. Therefore, it is important to gain followers who may be possible customers thereby building value for your business. Gaining followers on Instagram is not as difficult as on other social media platforms such as Facebook and Twitter since Instagram recommends who to follow based on your contact information or Facebook business page once you are done setting up your account. Once you follow users, they will follow you back if your brand is relevant to their needs or demands. Additionally, Instagram notifies your Facebook contacts on Instagram once you set up an account, therefore, it can help drive followers, but you should have other strategies of gaining followers as we are going to discuss below. With over ten thousand followers, you can monetize your Instagram account using several approaches as we will discuss later. First, lets us look at strategies you can use for your Instagram business account to gain over ten thousand followers.

1. Use right hashtags

As mentioned earlier, hashtagging your photos and videos is vital in ensuring you expand your audience by growing your following, as it makes it straightforward for users to locate and view your photos or videos after searching for specific names or hashtags. By using the right hashtags to tag your content, it's more likely that your account or product is easily discoverable by new users.

Finding the most relevant hashtag to tag your content can be hectic, and therefore you can use online tools such as Websta or IconoSuare. These tools enable you to find related and popular hashtags for your brand as they indicate the number of times a hashtag has been used. Note that Instagram allows a maximum of 30 hashtags per post, therefore, you have a wide category of hashtags to choose from. Additionally, you can steal hashtags from similar accounts or your competitors, but it is not advisable as you would want to create a relatable group of hashtags specific to your account. There are several ways to create hashtags for your brand such as Brand keyword Hashtags – #mybrandname, #fashion, #menswear. Product category hashtags – #socks, #happysocks, #sockswagg. Specific location hashtags – #LA, #LAfashion, #LAtrends, and so much more.

You can also use hashtags on your Instagram stories by using Hashtag stickers to increase the chances of a user following a specific hashtag view your story. Always try to be creative and use the most popular hashtags to attract users who in turn will follow your account if they are interested in your brand.

2. *Post Regularly and at the Right Times*

Do not falter from regularly posting photos and videos of your brand as consistency is key. Note that your followers do not follow you because of a past post, but because they are anxiously awaiting your future post making them tap on the following button. Posting regularly will ensure you have a consistent news feed which has a great impact on growing your followers as it entices any new follower to land on your profile.

Also, timing your posts is essential in reaching out to a larger audience who in turn may follow your account. There are various tools to establish the best time for posting, such as IconoSuare, which analyses your posting history vs user engagements and generates a report. The report establishes the best time of the day and days of the week for you to post content relating to your brand.

Attract your Competitors' followers to your Account

This is one of the best ways to gain followers as your competitor's followers have already expressed some level of interest in the same line of product, therefore, you can easily convince them to choose your brand over the competitor's product. One way to attract your competitor's followers is by engaging them at a personal level. On Instagram, there are three main types of engagements which are: following a user, commenting on a photo, and liking a photo or video. After engaging your competitor's followers by following them, liking and commenting on their photos and videos, it is almost certain that they will follow you back and comment on the content you have posted, thereby you gain followers in the process.

3. Sponsor Posts and Product Reviews by Paying

Influencer marketing on Instagram has been proven effective in gaining followers by exposing your brand to a broader audience. Although you pay for your posts to be shown to a larger audience, it is worth the cost as you will be able to gain followers at a faster rate when compared to other strategies if carried out correctly.

To sponsor a post, you should first identify accounts with numerous followers and within your product line. For instance, if you deal with men's fashion, establish accounts for men fashion bloggers with lots of followers. Contact the account owner using an email address that is usually provided on the bio and ask them to post your brand after agreeing on the sponsored post price. It usually ranges from $20-$100 per post depending on the number of followers.

In the case of an original product, you should consider sending them your product to post after reviewing. An example of a product review would look like these "I just got this perfect Tuxedo from @torontotrends and it's stylishly designed. Get yours here www.torontotrends.com." Users are then able to inquire about your brand since the post would appear more natural compared to a common advertisement which may sometimes be deemed misleading. In choosing influencers, select the ones with high engagement ratings rather than the ones with large followers but not engaging their followers.

4. Utilize Geotags for Easy Discoverability.

Geotags allow users to discover the location of your business after viewing your posts or stories coupled with a geotag. Location attracts followers just in the same way a hashtag does as users in a location or city can easily relate to your business to obtain products they might need urgently. Local businesses get the most out of location tags by regularly posting using the same location tag and interacting with posts from potential customers who may be in the same location as the business.

5. Categorize your Stories into Highlights

The "Highlights" feature enables you to convince a prospective customer visiting your profile to buy your brand in the shortest time possible. It is therefore necessary to categorize your Instagram stories using the" highlight" feature to effectively communicate what your account is all about. Stories have a 24-hour lifespan and may not be viewed by all your followers. Therefore, highlights will come in handy in to ensure all your followers view your brand Stories and even attract other followers to follow your account for future posts of your brand.

You can use Story Highlights to

- Develop short videos (trailers) on upcoming products with more enhanced features to give your followers a sneak peek into the upcoming product
- Arrange your Stories into themes in which your followers can easily relate to.
- Explain your products through videos and pictures.
- Promote your products using swipe-up links, which direct your followers to your website or wherever you would want to direct them.

6. *Organize a giveaway*

A giveaway organized occasionally is efficient ensuring you gain followers and expand the market for your brand. Through giveaways, users tag their friends or other users in the comment section to win the giveaway, which may be in the form of small rewards such as watches or cash rewards. The tag contributes to your post's engagements perfect for an Instagram algorithm, which in turn promotes the account to other users. Also, each tag fetches a new user who might be interested in your brand, therefore you could easily win them over to follow your Instagram business account.

It is also important to follow Instagram guidelines in running a promotion to avoid legal issues which might be costly for your business.

By using the strategies listed above, you should get more than ten thousand followers who you can monetize to gain additional funds from your account. It is important to note that Instagram by itself does not generate revenue, therefore you will need to use other strategies to monetize your account and generate revenue based on the number of your followers, as we are going to discuss below.

Ways to Monetize Your Instagram Following

What do you do with over ten thousand followers? As mentioned above, there are several ways to monetize your followers and turn them into a financial success. Strategies such as becoming an Instagram influencer, starting an e-commerce business or launching a social media consultancy firm have proven effective in turning your followers into financial success.

1. *Instagram Influencer*

Instagram influencers use some form of influence to make users prefer a brand over the rest of the products. Influencer marketing has gathered pace and is currently preferred by international brands such as Mercedes, KitchenAid, and Reebok who set funds aside to pay Instagram influencers. A study established that almost 95% of marketers regard influential marketing on Instagram as the best marketing strategy with a proven record of accomplishment in boosting sale volume.

Becoming an Instagram influencer enables you to monetize your large Instagram following and earn revenue from your account.

2. *Open a Social Media Marketing Firm*

With a huge Instagram following, you can start a social media consultancy firm in which you can earn enormous revenue by recommending social media marketing strategies to international brands. However, starting a social media marketing firm may be challenging, therefore you would need to start with developing small brands through direct messaging or email provided in their profile info on Instagram.

Similarly, you can start a social media company where you monetize your followers by selling ad space to other companies or brands rather than selling your own service or products. Also, the media company can be used as an Instagram channel to broadcast content to the target audience.

3. Partner with other Brands to Open an e-commerce Store.

An e-commerce store will exceedingly be successful on Instagram as your followers who may be prospective customers may be attracted to your brand upon viewing it. Instagram is suitable for e-commerce as your brand is not susceptible to enormous competition seen in Google search engine due Search Engine Optimization where your brand may end up generating low sales due to a small number of visitors accessing your page. The idea of Instagram marketing is to generate lots of followers who may be prospective customers and may end up buying your product. Furthermore, Instagram business tools such as "buy now" on the advertising button is significant for e-commerce. By partnering with other brands and launching an e-commerce platform on Instagram, you earn commissions from the sale of any product on your Instagram business account.

4. Sell Content to your Followers

With a huge number of enthusiastic followers, you can sell well-developed content such as movies, documentaries, or even a music video or album, thereby earning revenue. Instagram is a great platform to distribute your content by encouraging your followers to buy it or redirecting them to view it on YouTube through a posted link in the bio. You just post a trailer for your content and redirecting your followers to go view or purchase it.

5. Carry out Surveys for other Companies or Brands.

Instagram has a "poll" feature in which you can analyze the preferences of your followers. When companies want to launch a new product, they must survey the existing market to establish features they should add to the new product. Therefore, with huge followers, you might be contacted by the company to carry out a market survey, thereby earning revenue. Additionally, in the case of a company's Instagram account, the followers who take part in the survey may become some of the initial customers.

Chapter 3: Going Viral

Going viral on Instagram is important to grow your Instagram audience, thereby reaching out to prospective customers essential for the survival of your business. Additionally, going viral will create an impression among your followers who would eventually trust the legality of your business and purchase your brand.

How do you go viral?

There are several strategies you can use to go viral such as using popular hashtags or doing shout-outs, but it may be technically challenging for your posts to go viral on Instagram. The viral success of a post depends on delighting the Instagram algorithm's whose sole function is to deliver the best post to attract users to use the platform more often. By doing so, you, in turn, enhance the rate of engagement with your followers or other Instagram users who end up re-posting your post going viral. Additionally, going viral depends on the number of followers, quality of followers, and account automation, all of which increases the chances of your account being featured under "Explore tab," which is imperative for your account to go viral. Some of the approaches that you may use for your account to go viral are discussed below.

1. *Post Quality Content*

As mentioned above, quality content delights Instagram algorithms making your account go viral. Quality content may be in the form of graphically enhanced photos or videos and even memes which have proven effective in making your account go viral. The thing with memes is that they capture a users' attention as they can relate with the content in real life situations, therefore I would personally advise you to utilize memes in marketing your brand as it is very effective in ensuring your account goes viral.

You may also follow viral accounts and turn on post notification to see the latest memes or trendy topics then edit and repost the memes using the same hashtag in a way to market your business or brand. By doing this, your account will go viral in no time.

2. *Use Viral Hashtags.*

We discussed the importance of hashtags in our earlier discussion. There are tools such as Websta which you can use to find viral or popular hashtags. Appropriate hashtags will enable your content to be featured in Instagram explorer rather than the "Top Posts" section, thereby enabling your account to go viral and gain more followers.

3. *Timely Posting*

By using the Instagram analytics feature, you are able to identify the best time to post your content when your followers or other users are most active on Instagram. Timely posting is vital for your account to go viral as it increases the chances of engaging your followers through the post's comment section. In so doing, your followers may tag other users who might end up following your account or purchasing your product.

4. Establish your Niche.

For your content to go viral, you should study your niche to give you an idea what content to post that could possibly go viral. For instance, find out why a particular post elicited a reaction from your followers or why a post gained the most likes among all your posts. Establishing your niche will enable you to customize a post to match the desires of your followers and even attract new followers, making your account go viral.

5. Use Growth Hacks.

Some of the strategies we have mentioned above may require you to complement them by using growth hacks which have been proven successful in making an account go viral. Growth hacks such as Powerlikes work by altering the Instagram algorithm, increasing the rate of engagement and interaction with your followers and other Instagram users. When your post receives lots of likes within a short period, it will be featured under the "Explore Tab" where it will easily amass followers, thereby making your account go viral.

It is important to understand that not all content you post will go viral. The rule with virality is that your content should always be aggravating to elicit engagement with your followers. Your account will grow immensely once it goes viral, it is perfect for your business marketing.

Chapter 4: Instagram DM Groups

Instagram DM groups, also referred to as Instagram engagement groups, are used by Instagram users to engage among themselves through:

- Commenting and liking each other's post
- Viewing each other's Stories
- Commenting or replying to each other's Story timeline

Basically, Instagram engagement groups are aimed at driving more comments, likes, and followers to accounts in the group thereby steadily growing them. As we discussed earlier, for your account to grow, Instagram's algorithms must categorize your posts as being prevalent and place in the "Top Posts" section which can be achieved through Instagram engagement groups. Most Instagram DM groups are created on Instagram with others found on Facebook, Telegram, WhatsApp and other social media platforms. Depending on the engagement group.

How do Instagram DM Groups work?

Instagram engagement groups work in a very simple way referred to as "like for like" strategy. Instagram accounts with almost the same number of followers are pooled together in a group either on Instagram, Telegram, Facebook, and other forums. On joining such groups, you are obliged to engage in all videos and photos uploaded by members of the group to their Instagram accounts by liking, commenting, and tagging your followers or other Instagram users. In return, your account will be engaged with other similar accounts through likes, comments, and tags leading to spectacular growth through or following.

Joining Instagram DM Groups

Instagram DM groups are closed groups operating in secret. Therefore, it may be challenging to find and join a group. However, you can join these groups by sending a direct request (DM) to the group owner or a member of a group you would like to join. Usually, Instagram DM groups have different rules for enrolling new members. Some would charge you a small fee for joining while others are free and would require your active participation in liking and commenting on all photos or videos posted within the group. To locate these groups, you can use search engines, notably Google, as some are found on online forums or blogs of Instagram influencers. It is worth noting that Instagram engagement groups take time to grow your account, therefore you must be patient and dedicated to achieving success. There are two types of engagement groups, both of which are discussed below.

DM Groups on Instagram

These are the most common types of engagement groups and are usually found on Instagram. When a member uploads a new post to their Instagram account, he/she notifies the group members through a DM. Each group member must then engage in the published post by liking or commenting on the post as soon as possible. Similarly, before you can post, you must have engaged other members' posts. The comments and likes gained from group members assist in enhancing engagement and visibility of your account on Instagram, which is vital in gaining new followers.

Instagram Groups on Telegram

Instagram groups on Telegram operate correspondingly to DM groups, however, they have several key differences. First, they are hosted on Telegram and have thousands of members. The group is structured in a way that members can publish posts at specific time "rounds" rather than post sporadically throughout the day. This is to ensure that every post gets maximum engagement from the group members, thereby you are assured of account growth. Additionally, you get to choose which time "round" when you are most active on Instagram to post and you are not indebted to recover a period you missed posting or you did not participate in the group.

PRO TIP: Choose Telegram Engagement Group over Instagram DM Groups.

Telegram Engagement groups are much more effective in growing your account compared to Instagram DM groups. The Instagram algorithm "pleased" when a post gets more engagements at a faster rate, which can easily be achieved through Telegram engagement groups and may not be the case with Instagram DM groups since your post gains likes and comments intermittently rather than once. Also, Instagram DM groups are restricted to 15 people per group, thereby it may not be effective in generating enough engagements to grow your account. With a high engagement rate, your account will be featured on the Explore Page where it will be displayed to a much wider audience who may end up following you.

Chapter Five: Branding, Selling & Buying Accounts

Branding Instagram Accounts

The main aim of branding is to create an emotional connection between a business and its consumers. This is achieved through a combination of several marketing elements such as brand name, colors, logos and more. Branding enables a business to differentiate itself in a crowded market. On Instagram, it is possible to brand your business through visuals (visual branding). A strong Instagram branding is key to achieving success in marketing your business through Instagram. The thing with branding your account is that you should ensure that your overall business branding matches perfectly with the content you would want the target audience to view. For instance, if your brand employs lots of bright colors, so should your uploaded content. Here are some tips for branding your account.

Always Upload Beautiful Content

Beautiful content is the key to branding as it draws the attention of users to your brand. Your target audience will have first-hand experience with your visual representation and this will determine whether they will follow your account or even inquire about your brand, therefore, your content must be great. If you are unable to take high-quality photos of your brand, there are lots of copyright-free images where you can find beautiful high-quality photos. Additionally, you should ensure uploaded photos are clear, have high contrast and are well lit. You can also try uploading photos coupled with text to catch the attention of your audience and tell a story using visual items.

Uniformed Instagram Appearance

It may be challenging to take astonishing photos and upload them on a constant basis, but consistency is vital for visual branding. Strategize on the appearance of your Instagram account, whether you would want your brand to be vintage, classy, romantic or dramatic, always be consistent. You can use Instagram filters to enhance your images and get the emotional attention of your audience. Instagram filters such as Juno, Lark, and Clarendon increases the contrast of your posts while Reyes, Crema and Gingham make photos appear more pale and subdued. Photoshop software can also be used to achieve the best results for uniformity of your posts.

Tag your Post with Unique Hashtags.

As discussed earlier, hashtags make your post easily searchable, thereby exposing them to a larger audience. Additionally, hashtags elicit engagements among your audience, marketing your brand in the process. You should use at least two hashtags per post that are unique to your brands such as the name of your business or brand name. Unique hashtags are a simple way to increase the familiarity of your audience with your brand and is vital especially in branding a newly opened business.

Buying and Selling Instagram Accounts

Just like domain names and websites, Instagram accounts can be traded, although it is against their terms of services. As per Instagram terms of services, you are restricted to "sell, license, transfer or assign your accounts, followers, usernames and other account rights to any other user." Therefore, an authentic way buy accounts is not available and you should be careful when buying accounts as they are mostly filled with scammers. However, if you wish to buy an Instagram account for your business, there are available forums where Instagram accounts are advertised, and you can contact a broker to buy the account. Again, be very careful when buying accounts from these forums as they clearly state that buying accounts is at your own risk

The other option in buying accounts is to explore accounts advertising themselves for sale on Instagram.

Instagram accounts can advertise themselves for sale just like domain names and you can contact the account owner through a DM or an email that is usually provided in the bio. It is important to close the transaction face to face to avoid being defrauded of your hard-earned cash.

eBay also offers a platform where you can buy Instagram accounts and is a safer platform. However, recently eBay has stopped advertising accounts for sale on their platform as it is against Instagram terms of services and could lead to hefty fines.

There are also account selling sites such as Viral Instas and Fameswap where you could buy accounts from. From reviews, these platforms seem legit and you can safely buy accounts from them. Additionally, the accounts come with a manual on how to grow and maintain the account using some strategies we discussed earlier. They also come with a hashtag research app containing more than five hundred hashtags related to each page and the contents best suited for an account based on the followers or audience.

Selling an Instagram account may be challenging given by the fact that is against Instagram terms of services. However, it depends on the niche. For instance, if your account is based on hotel niche and your followers are food lovers, you can approach a hotel online and sell your account to them. You can also advertise on your account bio such as "Account for sale, contact: sale@email.com."

Instagram account buyers mostly look for the following things before buying an account

- Account name – Instagram accounts with shorter names are preferred by account buyers and are worth more, especially a "brandable" username. Copyright accounts pretending to be a celebrity account or accounts with long names are usually shunned by new buyers.
- Account engagement – Accounts with not only many followers but also their engagement such

as liking and commenting on a post are preferred by most buyers as they are sure of continuous growth and even worth more compared to inactive accounts

- Account Niche – Account niche defines the types of your followers and is an important factor in determining the price of an account. Common account types that deal with memes, funny videos, vines and other content are worth less and may not be effective in marketing your brand. Accounts dealing in products such as cars, gadgets, fashion, fitness and other content of the same nature are worth more and can easily market your brand.

It is hard to determine the real worth of an account looking at statistics or insights, but the general rule should be 0.50-3.00USD per a thousand followers based in Europe, Australia, Canada and North America. Remember always sell your account in secret away from the public eyes as Instagram can suspend any account they establish has been sold. Be careful not to give out your account login details before being handed the payment, as you can easily be swindled.

Chapter Six: Instagram Stories, IG Live, and Call to Action

Instagram Stories

Instagram Stories are a way of sharing videos and photos with your followers. The stories automatically disappear from your feed or profile after 24 hours unless you add a story highlight. Instagram Stories are a great way to market your brand as you can reach a wider audience using the stories (digital storytelling) in about 10 to 15 seconds. It is proven that Stories attract users to visit the platform more often and stay active for quite a long time. In November 2017, Instagram reported that the story feature had reached more than 300 million daily users. Therefore, you can easily market your brand given by the number of daily visitors.

Stories have become a popular way in which a business can promote their brands by sharing information outside their account feeds to reach a wider audience. Below are some ways you can use the story feature to market your brand.

Establish a Brand

A brand differentiates your brand from the rest of the products in the highly competitive market. By using Instagram Stories, you can create a brand by creating attractive content-rich stories. Always include a recognizable logo or any feature unique to your business when uploading to stories as it enables your followers to easily recognize your brand. You can also establish a brand using your stories by employing graphic design and including certain color schemes, color tone and font choice unique to your overall business branding. Through blending your Instagram stories with your account post and business websites, it creates a consistent unique look important for online marketing

Use your Stories to Get Feedback

A "poll" feature has been incorporated into Stories which can be a great way to get feedback from your customers. The questionnaires are overlaid on images and can easily initiate a prospective customer to give an honest opinion concerning your brand which is vital for marketing. Feedback is important in market research and will enable a business to find out whether a product is correctly satisfying its users in a way it was intended or what additional features can be added to increase customer satisfaction. Incorporating feedbacks to your stories is an inexpensive way to survey your brand's market.

Increases Interaction

Through Instagram stories, you can grow your account by interacting with your followers. You can do this by setting up contests through Stories, with an option to feature one of your followers in your story as an incentive or a fun prize. Stories offer an opportunity for your brand to grow and you may employ fun stuff, playful games relating to your niche, but remain professional. Always add popular hashtags to your stories as it encourages interaction with your followers who may be prospective customers.

Share Information about your Brand

Stories can be a great way to spread your brand information such as products designs, features, and specifications through visual images. Also, business information such as opening hours or offers and discounts can be shared through Instagram Stories. You may consult interactive media experts to come up with elegant stories to spread your brand information. However, you should not overdo with the text and focus more on photos and videos. You can add more information on your stories by providing a link where users can access more information about your brand by swiping up and will be redirected to an information source such as a website.

Advertise Events and Promotions

Instagram Stories offers an opportunity to share upcoming events or promotions in your business. The stories can include videos or pictures of ticket sales or discount prices with a link provided for online purchase. This, in turn, will be viewed by your followers who may be interested in the event or promotion thereby buying your brand.

When effectively used, Instagram can greatly improve sales of your brand as it disseminates your brand information in a visually appealing way.

IG Live

The Instagram live feature enables users to broadcast live videos using the app like Twitter's Periscope and Facebook Live where videos are shared in real time. Instagram Live works by streaming real-time videos via Instagram Stories. Unlike Twitter's Periscope and Facebook Live, IG live videos are automatically deleted after each live session and are not hosted on users' feeds. IG live videos do not have a time limit and can be used to market your brand effectively by creating a deeper connection with your followers who may be your potential customers using the following strategies.

Interact with your Follower through Live Q&A Sessions

Through IG live, you can interact with your customers by answering their questions in real time. IG live is designed in such a way that it is both an engagement platform enhanced by a simultaneous video broadcasting feature. Therefore, users can use a live chat to interact with hosts and other viewers through a comment section at the bottom of the screen. Viewers can ask questions, share thoughts and react to the videos via "like" feature. Through the live interactive sessions, you can clarify issues relating to your brand and analyze the thoughts of your customers by viewing comments. By doing this, you build trust with your customers, thereby boosting your brand sales volume.

Make sure you inform your customers when you would be hosting a live Instagram interactive session so that they may find the time or send questions relating to your business in advance via a Direct Message.

Broadcast a Demo, Class, Unboxing or Tutorial.

Use the Instagram live sessions to show your customers how your products or services work, configured or installed via live demos, unboxing videos, classes, and tutorials. Instagram live videos are not limited to time like Instagram posts or stories, therefore you can broadcast long video sessions showing the workability of your product and engage with your customers by answering live questions. For example, fitness instructors can broadcast live workouts and classes. Same goes for cosmetic companies or makeup artists who can broadcast live makeup tutorials or their products in use, and so many other services and products.

Broadcast "how it is made"

Let your audience take a sneak peek at how your product is manufactured or a behind-the-scenes look at your operations. This creates a good impression on your audience who may easily purchase your product. For instance, demonstrate the making of your product, a sneak peek of upcoming products, or even show customer's faces behind your business in the office.

The good thing about IG live is that the videos are not posted on your wall where you do not have to worry about inconsistency in your feed which can greatly affect your online marketing efforts.

Call to Action on Instagram

On Instagram, "call to action" refers to directing visitors to perform an action such as clicking on a link to visit your webpage. Calls-to-Action(CTAs) have a role in directing people in what you would want them to do after viewing your post or stories. You can ask your followers to buy your product, visit your website or interact with you through Direct Messaging. You must be creative when posting a call to action to attract your audience to take the action you have requested of them. Here are some ways you can be creative in posting a call to action, make your followers take the action, and market your brand in return.

Tease Your Audience

You can tease your followers prior to launching a product as it's an effective marketing strategy. The audience will be anxious to see the new product and would respond to the call-to-action effectively. The call-to-action should direct them to your business websites or stories to view a sneak peek of the product and may pre-order the product if interested.

Request your Followers Tag their Friends

You can creatively use call-to-actions to encourage your followers to tag their friends who may be prospective customers, thereby increasing your brand's market.

Additionally, tagging friends is a great way to grow your engagement which increases the chances of your account going viral and gaining more followers and furthermore increasing sales of your brand.

Employ Persuasive Language.

Phrases like "register now," "buy now" and "subscribe to" are persuasive phrases that can easily persuade your audience to respond to your call-to-action request. Therefore, you should always use such terms when creating a call-to-action on your Instagram account.

Inject Urgency in your CTAs

Always generate a sense of urgency in your CTAs as they make the consumer feel that they are missing something, provoking them to respond to the call. CTAs like "call now" creates a sense of urgency compared to "call soon." Phrases such as "limited time only," 'discount available for the first 20 buyers," "order within 24 hours to get discount code" and many more would incite your followers to make an order instantaneously and increase your sales volume.

Combine your CTAs with Attractive Pictures

Attractive photos catch the attention of your followers and can easily be convinced to respond to the CTA. Always insert texts in your photos and make them as visually attractive as possible by employing filters or photoshop software.

PRO TIPS:

- Employ the use of arrows pointing to the provided link
- Use emojis preferably the star, fire, and hand pointing emojis
- Paste the provided link after a CTA.

Chapter Seven: Affiliate Marketing through Instagram

One of the easiest strategies to monetize your followers and make money with your Instagram account is through affiliate marketing. Instagram offers a platform for affiliate marketing and you can freely signup, just ensure that your account has the massive following to be successful in the marketing process. There are several affiliate marketing programs you can choose such as car parts, online courses, electronics, fashion, and so much where you market these brands to earn commission depending on the type of your followers(niche).

Most people confuse affiliating marketing with multi-level marketing(MLM) which are basically Ponzi or Pyramid schemes. Ponzi schemes generate income for their founders by acquiring new investors who invest their cash and earn by gaining other investors progressing the scheme. Unlike Ponzi schemes, Instagram affiliate marketing involves marketing or selling a product on behalf of a company, earning a commission in return.

The payments differ depending on the signed agreement between you and the company in question. Some companies will pay you a commission from a subscription fee on every signup while others will pay you an agreed fee upon driving a certain number of signups. Therefore, you should clearly understand the demographics of your audience to make the most out of affiliate marketing.

Affiliate Marketing on Instagram

The largest E-Commerce company in the world, have an affiliate program which is very popular on Instagram and even the web. Joining the affiliate program is free and involves posting pictures of your affiliate products on your Instagram account and captioning it with call-to-actions requesting your followers to follow the link on your bio to purchase the product, coupled with appropriate popular hashtags. When your posts get most engagements or sales, you get a commission. However, Instagram limits the number of clickable web links you can provide on your bio to only one, limiting your market by:

- Limits your reach to prospective customers
- Limits you from posting multiple products

Nevertheless, tools such as elink.io enable you to put up several links on your Instagram bio thereby solving this problem, and enables you to earn commission from multiple sells.

In affiliate marketing, always post simple attractive images with some selling features such as the warranty. Always include colorful bold text such SALE, DISCOUNT, OFFER and SWIPE UP which will redirect your followers to the website to purchase the product.

PRO TIP:

Always post amazing products that you think can be afforded and fit your followers' lifestyles as they would easily buy it. Include a product review website LINK on your bio or on your Instagram Story.

Chapter Eight: How to Make Money with Shoutouts

Shoutouts is the other way you can monetize your numerous followers and generate revenue from your Instagram account. Shoutouts involve being contracted by a business or an account owner to market their brand to your followers who must be of the same niche with contractor's followers. For instance, a company dealing in men's fashion may not have enough followers on their Instagram page and would want to increase the visibility of their brand. Your account has a huge Instagram following, mostly men who may be prospective customers to the fashion brand. Therefore, the company will pay you to post some of their fashion brands on your Instagram account to be viewed by your followers.

Additionally, you may have to post a call-to-action requesting your followers to follow the brand's Instagram account and get paid in return. Shoutouts have recently become an effective way of making money on Instagram with establishing Instagram accounts with over hundred thousand followers generating thousands of dollars by endorsing brands through their Instagram accounts.

Companies are spending lots of money on buying shoutouts as Instagram reported that over four billion dollars were used in 2016 to buy shoutouts, as it's an effective marketing strategy. You can also make money from shoutouts on Instagram by mentioning fellow Instagram marketers on your posts who will pay you in return. However, you should make sure that your shoutouts stay within the needs of your audience. Overdoing shoutouts can lead to loss of followers as it commercializes your account which is usually overlooked by your followers.

How Much Money can you Generate per Shoutout?

Prices per shoutout vary widely depending on your Instagram following base, followers' engagement level, and your account niche. The most common price per shoutout is about $0.5 per thousand followers, which can generate lots of money monthly.

How Effective are Instagram Shoutouts?

When used correctly, Instagram Shoutouts can be very effective in gaining followers and in marketing a brand. When your business contracts well-established Instagram accounts for shoutouts, the brand will be viewed by a larger audience who may end up buying your brand thus boosting sales. Instagram shoutouts are more effective and less costly in marketing a brand compared to buying followers who may not be interested in your brand or are low-quality followers.

Chapter Nine: Best Apps to Use to Market your Brand on Instagram

With Instagram marketing gathering pace, application developers have not delayed in coming up with sophisticated apps to enhance your posts and market your brand effectively. The apps are categorized as Photo editing apps, graphic design apps, Instagram management apps, and video making apps. Below are some of the best apps.

Best Photo Editing Apps

As discussed earlier, all your post needs to be awesome for you to market your brand effectively. Photo editing apps will enable you to come up with amazing posts by adding filters, adjusting contrast and brightness, and removing any undesirable objects in the background. Here are some of the best Photo editing apps.

- ***VSCO Cam*** – This is a very popular, powerful photo editing app found on both Android and iOS platforms. The app has lots of free filters to choose from in addition to other filters which can be purchased.

- ***Snapseed*** – Developed by Google, this photo editing app is perfect for editing out specific areas of your photo. The filters may not be perfect, but the editing tools are very powerful enabling you to come up with attractive photos.

- ***A Color Story*** – It is good for creating colorful photos that can easily grab a user's attention. This was specifically designed to enhance color brightness on posts. A small number of filters are available and additional filters can be purchased.

- ***Line Camera*** – It is perfect for taking selfies for the personal branding of blogger accounts. The app maintains the quality of the image on the camera and can enhance your looks in no time.

You should, however, be careful while using the app to avoid embarrassing photoshop fails.

Best Graphic Design Apps

Graphic designs enable you to communicate the brand's message to your followers through the addition of text to your posts. They are easy to use and develops quality images for Instagram marketing. Here are some of the best graphic design apps.

- *Over* – The app is free and comes with features such as the cropping feature to crop your photos to required dimensions. Additionally, you can enhance a photo by adding opacity to a photo to make your texts appear clearly in the post. You can also download copyright free images using the app, add some text or artwork, and upload it to your account.
- *Quick* – Only available on iOS platform, Quick enables you to add texts to your photos.

It is perfect for adding a slogan or quote to your photos before posting. It has lots of great colorful fonts, great for visibility by your Instagram users.

Best Instagram Account Management App

These apps enable you to manage your account effectively by scheduling posts, tracking your engagement rate, and analyzing your feed. Here are some of the best Instagram management apps.

- *Iconosquare* – This app enables you to manage your account by tracking your account growth, engagement rates, and notifies you on the best time to post your brand where it will receive maximum views essential in marketing your brand. The app is available freely on a web page.
- *Latergramme* – This web app is essential for your Instagram marketing account. It enables

you to schedule posts on all your Instagram accounts, view your Instagram feed, and engage with your followers through the app. It also informs you of the best time to post through a push notification.

- *LiketoKnowIt* – It is designed for Instagram blogging accounts with the sole purpose of earning commission from followers who would like to adopt their account look. It notifies bloggers of a liked post who would then send the likers a link to buy the account looks.

Best Video Recording App

Instagram videos are a great way to market your brand by demonstrating the features or functionalities of your product. You should record and post high-quality HD videos to attract users to buy your brand. You can use these apps below to record high-quality videos.

- *Hyperlapse by Instagram* – This app is available on iOS and enables you to easily create a short video or time-lapse videos which can be posted on your Instagram account. The image stabilization features enhance the quality of your video that is usually affected by shaky hands.
- *iMovie* – It is available exclusively on iOS being a mobile version of the Mac video app. It enables you to improve the quality of your video through filters and by adding other video effects such as split-screen, slow motion, and even fast forward.

These are just some of the best apps I have sampled and there so many others that can enable you to manage your Instagram account more effectively.

Conclusion

From our discussions, it is evident that Instagram, when used correctly, can be an effective tool in marketing your brand. The rule on Instagram is to upload quality content over quantity to easily attract your audience who may end up purchasing your brand. Always engage with your followers to grow your account following and make your brand post go viral and reach a wider audience.

Use popular hashtags when posting as it ensures your posts are easily discoverable, important in marketing your brand. Employ Instagram features such as Instagram Stories and IG live to broadcast your product to your audience, thus marketing effectively. Instagram is seamlessly integrated with other social media platforms such as Facebook and Twitter and you can share your posts on these platforms to be able to reach a wider audience who may be prospective customers. Instagram accounts with numerous followers can generate revenue in several ways such as affiliate marketing, shoutouts, and selling accounts, although it's against Instagram terms of service. Always remember that branding, consistency, and quality are key to Instagram marketing.

I hope this book has been of great help in enabling you to learn Instagram for business and ways you can grow and monetize your followers. In this social media age, you should have a strong Instagram to effectively market your brand and at a cheaper cost.

Thank you for Buying this Book.

May I take this opportunity to thank you for purchasing this book. I would love to hear your opinion on this book and I am pleased that you have selected our company and bought this informative book. Please, check out other books in our collection, spanning different topics to be informed on online marketing trends.

www.ingramcontent.com/pod-product-compliance
Lightning Source LLC
Chambersburg PA
CBHW070116230526
45472CB00004B/1286